BAGS AND TOOLS

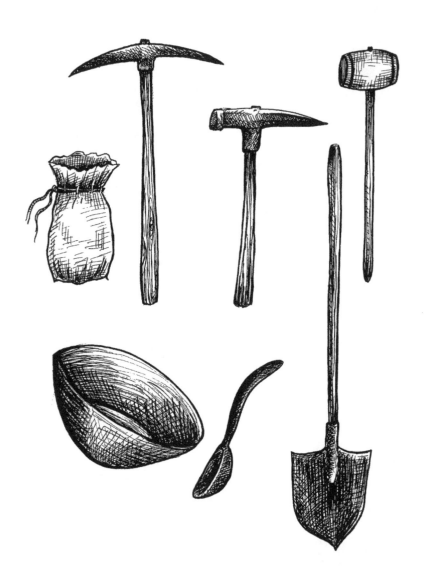

BAGS
AND
TOOLS

Poems

Michael Fleming

With Illustrations by Frances Cannon

GREEN WRITERS PRESS | *Brattleboro, Vermont*

Printed in the United States

10 9 8 7 6 5 4 3 2 1

Green Writers Press is a Vermont-based publisher whose mission is to spread a message of hope and renewal through the words and images we publish. Throughout we will adhere to our commitment to preserving and protecting the natural resources of the earth. To that end, a percentage of our proceeds will be donated to environmental activist groups. Green Writers Press gratefully acknowledges support from individual donors, friends, and readers to help support the environment and our publishing initiative.

Giving Voice to Writers & Artists Who Will Make the World a Better Place
Green Writers Press | Brattleboro, Vermont
www.greenwriterspress.com

Sundog Poetry Center, Inc.
Poetry for all Vermonters
www.sundogpoetry.org

ISBN: 978-1-950584-84-0

Illustrations by Frances Cannon

COVER PHOTO:
"Pyrite" by Frances Cannon

The paper used in this publication is produced by mills committed to responsible and sustainable forestry practices.

for Marti

CONTENTS

FOREWORD

What compelled me about *Bags and Tools* was its reach for a "we." The "we" was open enough and varied enough to encompass a wide swath of people(s) but did not assume a sameness—indeed, it sought in part to elucidate the matter of difference through questioning. In "Dreams," Michael Fleming notes that "Their logic is not your logic," and then goes on to write ironically of the speaker's own "fine certitudes" that fail in the light of others' realities. This brings to mind Taha Muhammad Ali's line "My happiness is not your happiness," which immediately agrees upon happiness but insists upon its own terms while questioning the aims of others. It seems a simple observation, but it is not—it is nuanced and insightful.

Much of this author's work is the same, plain-spoken, but upon reading it presents its concerns. What is in the bag of the speaker who presents themself as a would-be vagabond, a wayward traveler? A curious mind, a passionate search for a larger framework (God, Love) through what the reader could think of as letters to beloveds as much as dedications where names are cited. This is a book I will read again, then again. It is the speaker's trying that I find so relatable. The skein is thin here, so author and speaker are close. Michael Fleming effectively uses the tools of craft to take us along on this narrow path that widens and promises to open into broad understanding.

—VIEVEE FRANCIS

BAGS AND TOOLS

I filled my bags with lumps of lead
and stumbled underneath the load,
and just when I was nearly dead
I met a beggar on the road.

He drew me near and shut one eye:
"Give me your lead, I'll give you gold."
I dreamed of all the things I'd buy
and left him there with what I'd sold.

My bags were lighter than before
but still my tired back was bent;
I found an ironmonger's store
and soon that shiny gold was spent.

And now at last I can begin
with iron tools of every kind;
I'll dig a hole and throw them in
and leave those bags and tools behind.

JUST A WORD

Casino

I hit the jackpot the night I met you.
Hell, what did I know from jackpots? The game,
the hard, hungry art of losing—I knew
that much. If I was driven by the same
neon dream as every other moth, what of
it? Who doesn't want to win? In my trance
of limitless blind desire and the love
of oblivion, I heard the gods of chance
murmuring *maybe next time, maybe next
time, maybe next time*—numbers hardly mattered.
And then they did. I should have expected
the savage, flashing red lights, the pratfalls
of victory, klaxons and bells, fat
men in shades and ill-fitting suits too tight
in the collar who came to me—a gaunt,
furtive escapee, caught in the spotlight
glare of getting everything I wanted.

Play Me the Blues

Play me the blues—oh God, play me the blues,
and make it the slow kind, in for the long
haul, the last of the light, make it a blues
that knows that I know, a little bit wrong,
a little bit home, and give me the blues
that earns a hard righteous dollar and spends
it because that's what dollars are for, blues
in the empty night, nothing to pretend,
nothing left to hide, give me last-call blues,
slow-grinding, come-to-Jesus, what-the-hell
blues about careless love and secrets, blues
that hurt just right, hurt me *here*, if I fell
for you it wouldn't even matter blues,
your tongue down my spine blues, the body wants
to feel something deep, something real, the blues
is what the body wants, it wants to dance,
it wants the pulse of blood and pain, it wants the blues.

Things Are Bad

Things are bad. The doors are unhinging, guardrails
are down, the birds have stopped singing, waters
are rising, hard rains are falling, hard
men have grabbed the reins, brainless wars are fought
over little-boy playthings, over tantrums,
tiny hands, wounded pride, peccadillos,
passing fancies, and meanwhile fire ants
and poison ivy rampage northward, killing
frosts creep southward, storm clouds gather westward,
plagues loom eastward, our constitution
is cracked, our spirits are snuffed, the best
have been shouted down by the worst, the blues
are back in town, it looks like we've been had—
trouble ahead.
           Like I said, things are bad.

Corona

In the beginning it was just a word—
some kind of bug, a blip in the news,
another ambient danger, like murder
and bad service and diaper rash—the dues
for being alive, one more thing to think
about. It began to cover the sun
and we said this isn't happening, sinking
into the sea isn't happening, none
of this is real, unpredicted eclipses
cannot occur, we will not allow
it. Then all at once night fell—time was stripped
of meaning, birds stopped singing in a cloudy,
starless sky. No hint of dawn. We must
have failed to see this coming, most of us.

We failed to see it coming, most of us,
because we never thought about the plague
or pestilence—antique notions we must
have forgotten. Now the enemy flag
flies everywhere, unseen, and we obey
or we disobey, and we calculate: Who
has it? Who is a vector? What have they
touched, breathed on? Everything we thought we knew
was wrong, delusional, a dream of climbing
an endless staircase made of sand, light
infected with darkness and distrust, time
turned viscous, like glue. Unending night,

silence. We long to tell ourselves: Spring came
so late this year, but it came all the same.

Spring came so late, but it came all the same—
we willed it to mean what it always means:
life! And the flowers still bloomed, and the names
we gave ourselves were names from what we'd been
before. We want freedom! But what *was* our
freedom? It's hard to remember—forgetting
comes so easily now, and the power
of the sun drives common sense away. Let's
pretend—it never happened. And that cough?
We never heard it. Even Jesus stumbled—
but then he got up! So let's ignore
it—it's gone, vanquished, and if time is off
its moorings, even old quarrels are something
to cling to. Anything from before.

Cling to anything from before—what else
do we know? The way we touched when our faces
were unmasked, unmistakable, wellsprings
of love, or the way we moved with grace,
determined and unafraid. We remember
dance floors, handshakes, running with the crowd,
packing the house, gathering and assembling,
forming congresses and choirs, and the loudest
voices sang in harmony, made sense
of suffering, made sense. Now we don't play

music together. All our monuments
are broken. Our masks are the price we pay
for breathing, venturing out. We were wrong
about so much. We were masked all along.

We were masked all along, and it took wearing
masks to know that. Now we look like what
we always were— midwives and bandits, caregivers
and surgeons, sneak thieves, desperadoes.
Who doesn't love a costume—we'd all
die of shame if our souls were bare! Today,
let's write a tragedy featuring pallbearers
with masks made of smoke, strutting playboys
with masks made of wasps, and in the last
scene we'll wear masks of love and loss and crimes
of passion, spirits with a special spark
of life, of danger. Con the lines. The past
is hardly prologue, and now it's showtime—
as the curtain rises, the house goes dark.

The curtain rises as the house goes dark—
suddenly everything goes wrong. We're all
naked, our masks hide nothing. When we call
out "line!" we get silence. We miss our marks,
forget our parts, plead with God. Someone coughs.
The director flails his arms, useless, impotent
to restore the illusion. Scrims
descend at random, the actors go off

script, a stagehand sniffs and whispers, *I smell*
smoke. The players improvise a fan dance
to hide our humiliation. Someone yells
and is shushed, the director starts to rant
about the music, it's all wrong because
singing is forbidden—it always was.

So—singing is now forbidden. It was
the thing we loved best in the beforetimes,
but now we're all in this alone. Who doesn't
want to dance again? Is it a crime
to make a little whoopee, make some noise,
make music in the midst of solitude?
We never knew how much we'd miss our voices,
the act of shaking hands, sharing food,
touching one another. The months unfold
without rhythm, without sequence— a fever
dream of silence flowing like a herd
of deer over a fence. It's getting cold.
We didn't want this. We couldn't believe
it at first, when it still was just a word.

Used to It

At first we were bewildered—words like *why*
still meant something to us then, and the stars
still spoke to us, we still looked to the sky

for answers. But we had so much to lose—
at first the losses hurt. We tried to buy
our way out, cast magic spells to confuse

it, make it go away, anywhere far
from here. But nothing worked, and we got used
to it— we had to. You know how things are.

Hunkering

They must be etymological friends,
hunch and *hunker*—by *hunch* I mean the verb,
not the noun, not the gambler's last pretense
of knowing the unknowable, disturbing
the universe, but rather the act
of drawing inward, making yourself small—
you're crouching, *hunched*, no target—and you've packed
your bags, just in case. And *hunker*? You wall
yourself in and hope for the best.

                                    I'm thinking
of Masada, how it was for them,
besieged, *hunkering*, gazing at the sinking
sun, the Roman camp below, remembering
everything they'd lost, the relentless
rising ramp and everything it meant.

What We Wanted

We wanted it to end in smiles, parades,
our enemies embracing us as friends,
as saviors, another cornerstone laid

in the temple of our greatness, our victory
garden. We wanted what we paid
for. We wanted more time, wanted to pick

the perfect moment, solemnly and gently
pulling the plug in the glow of flickering
candles. We wanted it to end.

Vichy

The reckoning came later, after lines
had been crossed, choices had been made that could
never be unmade—blood betrayals, signs
twisted toward the wrong roads. They had good

reasons—so it seemed at the time. *The war* . . .
they would mutter, after, their voices trailing
off vaguely, wanting to shut that door
and keep it shut—rebirth behind a veil

of clouded memory. Some felt the sting
of shame. Some lied until they could forget
they'd ever said yes, and kept fingering
their lies like rosary beads, silver chains set

with precious stones, polished to a dull shine
and mumbled in the small rooms where they sought
absolution. Some drowned their lies in wine
and smoke.
           The others, they never forgot.

In the Hot Seat

It's like you've been subpoenaed— you get grilled
about everything you know, everything
you did and what you meant, the room is filled
with paparazzi and you want a drink
but the water glass is just out of reach
beyond the bubble of light that surrounds
you. *Isn't it true?* demands a voice. Each
time you try to answer, all your words sound
like bird calls, like wind rushing through the trees,
a hard, merciless wind, and all you want
is some water, not these questions, these reasons,
these stories, these lies, these dust motes dancing
in the light, swirling like smoke . . . just some
water, you're thinking, or maybe a beer,
a cup of tea— you just want to go home.
Anything but this, anywhere but here.

The Anthropocene

They'll find the plastic, thick deposits everywhere,
and kids will comb through it to find
lighters and blades. The junkyards will be mined
for useful metals, all those Fords and Chevies
picked apart for lead and steel and screws,
the trophies of another time. *What happened?*
they'll ask, puzzling at the MAGA caps
and snowmobiles and fallen bridges, clues
to piece together, and the wise among
them, the seers, scholars, and poets, will explain
the past, but few will listen to their warnings
not to venture where dead trees are strung
with dead wires, in the deserts where the rains
failed while people feasted on their seed corn.

II

HINDSIGHT

The Merry Dancers

Misery is Canada. Loneliness
is a road in northern Ontario,
a road disappearing into black spruce
forever to the east, into the glow
of a failing sunset to the west, not
a single car to flag down, not a truck
pulling logs the size of ships, not a thought
of such a truck slowing, stopping . . . no luck
to be had, no driver to say, "Whatever
you do, don't get stuck in Wawa, eh."
Madness is blackflies, relentless, meat-driven,
stippling a white shirt fire-itch red. Plague
is a darkness thick with mosquitoes, clouds
of mosquitos, ear-seeking, infinite—
but—less infinite than the stars, or how
the sky's an ocean, breathing tides of light.

Hindsight

I lost my journal once, maybe in an airport
or on a train, back when I wrote my self, rejected
every other way. I had consulted fortune

tellers, written it down. I'd scribbled in tents
high on mountains, distant beaches . . . recorded courtships,
failures, theories of God—it all made no sense.

Decades passed. And then my journal came back, dissected,
sender unknown—each page annotated, densely
edited, everything made right and correct.

On the Bus

Life into legend, legend into life—
I once was you, Alex Supertramp—fresh
out of school, half nuts, no money, no wife,
no work, no matter. The sins of the flesh
were behind me, beneath me, beyond me.
Another self-inventing dharma bum
on the road to anywhere, off to see
the elephants, bound for glory. And from
such dry, dreary soil I'd sprung—I was you,
Alex—naked in my cast-off clothes, so
full of myself, so empty, just a few
well-tasted words were enough when the low
clouds to the west whispered, *Get on the bus,*
and I got on, and you got on—we wanted
more, magic, *furthur*, Alaska—I must
have crossed the river. But you? You were gone.

for Chris McCandless

Saint David's Head

In my defense, as I would later tell
myself, I was weary, footsore, alone.
I had no map—but no matter. The Welsh
moors, the Irish Sea beating on the stones
a hundred feet below—who needs maps? I
would take no rest, I resolved—not until
I reached Saint David's Head, and then I'd lie
on the grass beside the path, have my fill
of the wine I'd brought to help me admire
myself for arriving—the end of the world.
I conjured ghosts of murmuring druids, choirs
of angels as luminous as schoolgirls
to greet me, sing my song. But every time
I reached the farthest headland, there would be
another, farther still; each time the fine
spring day reproached me, mocked me. After three
such defeats I finally lost heart and let
myself collapse beside the path and chew
my onion vanities, watch the sun set
into the sea, drown in dark wine. In due
time I stood and stretched and watched a gull
hop effortlessly into the headwind,
hovering there in flightless flight, the pull
of gravity poised against the relentless
push of wind. And then I saw the trick—
the path bore right. The rocks I'd seen ahead—
an island. So this was where banshees shriek
at fools who've been here all along—Saint David's Head.

Pride

"We're proud here — *muy orgulloso.*" At first
I didn't understand, just thought I did,
each time they said so. Soon enough they burst
into mocking smiles — *"hombre,* just kidding"
is what I heard, what I meant to hear.
But that day in Algeciras, we snared
ourselves a table in that café near
the water, near the ferry that would carry
us to Africa. The place was packed
with laughing soldiers bound for empire's last
bastions, for Ceuta, for Melilla, back
from Easter with their mothers.

                                    It happened so fast:
a middle-aged and overburdened waiter
tripped on a luckless duffel bag, tried
to save himself, fell amidst crashing plates,
arose shining with tears, food, blood, pain, pride.

Math Teacher

Who is this stranger from across the sea?
He has no tribe, no sons, no cattle—how
can we respect such a man? What can we

learn from such a man? What can be his power?
Does he think his chalk's not a sjambok,
or that he's no fat, beer-swilling Boer? Now

he smiles—we fear his smiles. We fear his talk,
his laughter so unlike our own, his skin
called white but not white—no, white is a flock

of egrets bearing news from heaven, thin
elegant necks, plumes for the king—not pink
like this umlumbi ghost who broils in

the sun, looks like cooked impala tongue, stinks
like milk too long in the calabash. We
mistrust a man who tells us how to think.

One Perfect Day in New York City

Welcome to one perfect day in New York
City: a warm cotton-soft day, a cool
day, so good to walk, to glide through the air —
an unexpected day of grace when time
is not the enemy. Truly, a free
day, unclocked, unencumbered, off the books,

beckoning. A day like this is the book
you always wanted to read, and New York
is the author. Open it. Wander free
in its pages of dreaming streets, still cool
this morning, still unread. You have the time.
The city is quiet, traffic is light. Air

streams gently through the plane trees, golden air,
rich with the scent of fresh bagels, old books,
lingering perfume. Up Broadway to Times
Square, somehow the word is out, all New York
is in on the secret of this bright, cool
day, strangers smile slyly as they pass, free

of their strangeness, their hurry and fear, free
of their habits of unbeauty. The air,
the faces, the streets shimmer with a cool,
new-minted shine. Glancing up from their books,
people in buses smile slyly. New York,
this is your one perfect day, take the time

to love it. Ask anyone for the time,
the answer is yes; ask the price, it's free.
The museums are all open. "New York . . . ,"
you murmur, meaning all of it: the air,
the buildings, the faces, the streets, the books.
Even elevator muzak is cool

music on a magic day like this. Cool
jazz—a sax that knows its way around time,
when to bend it, when to go by the book,
when to open the cage of the sounds, free
to echo through the streets and fill the air
like doves on this flawless day in New York.

Soon the cool melodies shake themselves free
of time and lift us, rising in the air
above the books, and beauty, and New York.

Perfect

He slid the drink across the bar. *And that's*
what's called a perfect manhattan, my friend.
He stared, daring me to disagree. *Fat*
chance you'll find better anywhere else. Ten
dollars said he was right, said we could be
conspirators, real New Yorkers. I nodded,
took the glass, drank, nodded again. He
reminded me of something about God —
I got that much, and thought about the burning
light outside, and Second Avenue
melting beyond the heavy velvet curtains.
He poured another. Night fell like glue,
like hours oozing through hot asphalt, falling
ashes. He told me about his barn
swallow life, plastered to a canyon wall
in a nest made of mud and spit. He warned
me about the ones with money, the ones
without, the bridge-and-tunnel crowd with their
whoop-de-doo, their virulent hair, their guns.
He leaned a little closer. *But I care*
about this town, he said. *I'm like a fireman,*
saving people, saving their stuff, dowsing
the flames. Perfect. I said I was tired,
had to go. *One more,* he said, *on the house.*

Pedestal

First you noticed the beard—an Old World beard,
a patriarch's beard, and the eyebrows—wild, white,
alarming. And the fine blue eyes that peered
down from—where? Mount Gnosis by way of nights
around a glowing turf fire in Armagh,
or Cork, telling the stories, listening. He
made us want to be better people. So
one day, he happened to need a lift; me,
I just happened to have a car. The privilege
was mine. We were driving through the woods,
now sunny with the light that his eyes gave
off, and with the bright shine of all I could
do to be worthy of his smile, his friendship,
his view of life. Life! Yes, that was it—real
life we were discussing when the chipmunk
darted out, *bump-bump* under the wheels.

for Don Sheehan

Our Haloes

On the day that we gave ourselves haloes
our smiles were broad, bright, blinding, and we knew
that we were right. We watched as the sun rose
to perpetual noon, and in virtue
of our peerage we raised a glass or two.

On the night that we gave up our haloes
the moonlight shone on snow like windowpanes
and we wandered lost while the heavens froze
into useless constellations — we named
them, breathed their names, remembered why we came.

History

It got into everything, always did.
It clung to our hands, sucked at our feet, crept
into our homes, our beds, our food. The grit
of it broke our teeth. Even when we slept
we dreamed it—there was nothing else to dream.
Then the whispering began: *higher ground,*
as though we'd never thought of that. It seemed
impossible at first, but soon the sound
of those two words alone was all we heard—
higher ground. By day we followed the sun,
by night the stars. The wind was bright and stirred
our hearts. By God, we would not be outdone!
We drank and sang, we danced and fought. And then
we watched the clouds close over us again.

Mickey at the Rail

Done with it, he mutters when you ask him
what county, what town. The wind is so cold,
it smells of the sea and the smoke, the dim
light down in steerage, the reek of the old
woman puking in her apron— she won't
make it across, the same as lots of them.
Sick of life, that's what they are, no-counts,
he says. You ask him again, ask his name.
Mick — he starts to say, looking away, cuts
himself short. McGuire? McGuffin? But he's
got the chat in him if you press: an orphan
at fifty, no kid anymore, free
of the woman who left him, free of more
than that . . .
       He pulls at his cap, silent, stands
and stares at a hole the size of Ireland.

Grease Monkey

"Just don't let nothin scream," he says, and hands
me back my keys, a little tentative,
as if to say, "Oh sure, but can you *drive*
it?" Check or charge, it's all the same—the man
doesn't even care. At first, the car seems
strange as I head for home, minding the things
he told me—I barely let the engine sing,
I think about suffering, hear the screams,
and I baby the clutch, just brush the brakes, sip
the gas, progress noiselessly through the gears—
I never really go home at all.
                                    Years
later, same car, same old dog. We take trips
through the dark, into the forest, where he
cocks his ears at things I can't even see.

for Trooper

The Spoils of Jerusalem

A hundred times taken, the city gleams
with golden domes, whispered riches, the tides
of history. Conquerors have come, dreaming

of the Holy of Holies, the Rapture,
the Grail . . . of a never-ending stream
of loot. My plunder? A coffee-stained map,

some hard-bartered trinkets, two tattered guidebooks,
three shekels, and just a single snapshot
of God, before the battery died.

III

ONE OF US

Dreams

Man kindles a light for himself in the nighttime.

—HERACLITUS OF EPHESUS

Their logic is not your logic, their rules
are your shadow rules, the passions at play
unconstrained by what you thought to be true—
life reconsidered, life retrieved. By day
you shoulder your fine certitudes; like an ox
you submit to the yoke of everything
you've gathered as your burdens.
                           But night mocks
your certitudes, it flies in on bat wings
and stages weird little plays starring you
as yourself, works out the neurotheology
of your self, makes you play the fool
in every worst way—it watches you falling,
forever falling, falling . . .
                       Dear night,
blameless night, take me down into the foundry,
soot-black, steaming, where the only light
is the glowing molten slag all around.

Uncle in the Attic

He's up there — Uncle in the attic, under
the chimneypots. We hear him at night,
enraged at things we just can't see. We wonder
at his funhouse laugh, his schemes to brighten
up the dark, his incessant tap-dancing,
his unbecoming sense of command.
Sometimes he stomps down in his underpants
and shiny shoes to give us guff, demand
outlandish rents and whatever we've got
in the icebox. We don't trust him. We fear
his sulks, his quicksilver moods. When it's hot
he complains, and when it's cold. Does he hear
us when we laugh at him? Do we disturb
his dreams? Does he even sleep? All our noise
comes to nothing — we ate the magic herbs
that make us think, *This time he'll give us toys.*

Dreaming of Socrates

I see him in his toga, and he smells
like a foot soldier on campaign. He
laughs at my perplexity and he tells
me to hold it lightly. "Of course, you're free

to think otherwise," he says, and he laughs
some more. It starts to rain, and yet he stays
as dry as chalk. He says, "Someday I'll have
to . . ." and his voice trails off, and in his gaze

I see myself, my failings and my shame.
"No questions," I plead. "No method."
                                                    "So why
do you fear my questions?" he asks — the same
thing he asked me last time, and again I

have no answer. His hair begins to burn,
then his eyes, then his whole head is on fire
but unconsumed. He smiles a smile that turns
to smoke and everything's burning, everything's fire.

Hungry

All the conversations stopped when she said,
I've seen you hungry, and everyone knew
what she meant, and one of us thought of red
meat hissing over hot coals under blue
skies, and one thought of what it is to want
and how life is just want want want, and one
thought of hunger's nakedness, how it haunts
our dreams with raw shame, and one thought of guns
and what some people will do to survive,
and one thought of nothing because he'd never
been hungry, and one thought of the blessings
and miracles that keep us alive,
and one thought only in numbers, of seven
fires in seven bellies, more or less.

Space Walk

A vacuum, they assured me, pushing me
into the airlock, buckling on my
bubble head. Just that one idea—
nothing, the void, the great by and by.
Then nothing turned out to be everything,
and everything was music, swelling chords
of darkness-piercing light, every star singing
the song of fire! But those are just words—
what else to say when they reeled me in?
The words felt like stones revolving around
the dead suns of what I could never tell
them. All I could do was point at the spinning
cosmos, that vacuum filled with the sounds
they knew already— their heavens, their hells.

Aquinas Has Questions for Hakuin

. . . By this time he had lost his reputation, which did
not trouble him, but he took very good care of the child.

—PAUL REPS, *Zen Flesh, Zen Bones*

So when they came to you—the weeping girl,
her angry parents demanding to know
Was it you?—did you surrender? What pearl
were you hiding in your words *Is that so?*

And when they left the baby at your door,
did you name the child Falsehood even though
you loved her, bought her milk? Were you too poor
in spirit to say more than *Is that so?*

And when a year had passed and back they came
weeping for your forgiveness, did you show
them your wounds? They took the child—did you blame
them? Is that what you meant by *Is that so?*

Jubilee Blues

Anguish and grief, like darkness and rain, may be depicted;
but gladness and joy, like the rainbow, defy the skill of pen or pencil.

—FREDERICK DOUGLASS

The books were all about November— dying
light, brown withered leaves, black ink on white
paper, words to call the colors. And I
was sure I understood. By candlelight
I read about despair, and understood.
I read about freedom, too, and of love
and the words for its colors, and I could
recite those words. What did I know? Above
the wharf, above the masts, above the smoke
and stink and roaring might of New York, I
saw the sky for the first time, and the docks
were alive with free men in blue; the sky
was blue beyond my words, beyond my books—
I laughed with the men, and began to cry.

Amerigo Vespucci

The naming rights, it turns out, never seem
to go to the noblest, the first, the most
meritorious — not when we're naming dreams
and planting our flags, appeasing the ghosts
of what we fear. Who doesn't love a con
man? He said he'd been there—four times! He told
the best story—we loved it! On maps drawn
from memory we saw dragons and gold,
spices, condos glimmering in the sun—
such easy terms, such beaches! And what really
got us was the girls— so young, so free,
so naked, so unencumbered by shame
or by God. They're not like us. We aren't stealing
it, we're making it— this chance to be
something, to start with nothing but a name.

Damien of Moloka'i

They say we are cursed by God—that is why
the king sends his tax collectors to take
us away from our mothers, and they cry
"Unclean! Unclean!" when the first pustules break
the skin, and everyone knows what will come
in turn—the lost fingers and toes, the rot
and reek of walking death. We hear the drums
at night, remember life and what we're not.
It's true—we were luckless, lost, when he came.
We drank and fought and swore, we didn't care—
but he cared. He loved us and said we must
love ourselves, share our bread, drink from the same
cup—sick or strong, we all breathe the same air.
He said he came to become one of us.

Foxholes

When the time was right he told us about
the war—boredom, fear, and loneliness most
of the time, then terror and noise, and shouting,
screaming, the pop and heave of guns, ghost
moments that never go away and things
that cannot be unseen. *That's where I found
God,* he said—*where I found love, and the sting
of knowing what love means, how we're all wounded
and scared, doomed but still alive—alive!*
He told us about foxholes and bargains
with fate, grasping for anything to drive
away the onrush of death, make the pain
stop, hush the noise. *And I'm still in that war,
still in that foxhole,* he said—*we all are.*

for W. W.

The Birth of Language
(Reflections on Recycling Night)

Back in the caves, when we were showing off
our shiny new opposable thumbs
and tottering on our hind legs, enough
of us must have had the insight that some
stuff was worth holding onto, and some not—
decisions would have to be made. This stone,
that stick—keepers. But shattered sticks and rotten
meat and broken blades and blackened bones,
things whose very presence was burdensome—
into the midden. What need for words when
we stared into the embers, felt that odd
wonderment at the stars and where we come
from? No. The first useful word must have been
trash—before *tool*, before *fire*, before *God*.

Waiting in Line at the Liquor Store

That look we exchange in the liquor store —
it's all right there: shame, defiance, oblivion,
the love we've been denied. Let's ignore
the voice of the village scold, let's not give

ourselves up to the perp walk, flashing red lights
in the rearview, the deputy's soft knock
in the middle of the night, screaming fights,
the drunken uncle whose wine-crazy talk

ruins everything. I guess I agree: booze
leads to madness, sometimes in those who drink
and always in those who don't — those who choose
to scorn the devil's alchemy. But think

of it: money turned to spirits, America's
hardest-fought dollar in exchange
for song, friends, poetry, moments without care —
the loving cup, the lifted chalice, strangeness.

Don't I know you from somewhere? Wasn't I
that apeman in the cave of magic berries —
and you that apewoman wandering by,
she who grunted, *Fancy meeting you here?*

Ötzi

My father taught me how to hunt. He showed
me how to read the signs of bison, deer,
and ibex, to summon their spirits, know
their ways. He taught me how to know their fear,
their habits, their hungers. He taught me how
to make a bow from seasoned yew, a string
from sinews tightly wound. I learned about
the shining stone and how to work the things
we need—blades, scrapers, points for arrows. I
became a man before I had a beard,
and ventured far and wide, into the high
mountains, beyond where I should go, to where
the devils are—countless times I dared
to come here alone. This is where I die.

Rewilding the Golf Course

First come the wildflowers, the fairways bright
with bachelor buttons and forget-me-nots,
bluebirds perching on pin-flag poles. At night
the ponds are bordellos of peepers. Hot
winds whistle through the thickening stands of cactus
taking over the sand traps. The greens
are prairies — sweetgrass, bison. Bring it back,
let it all return to rough. Bring back eons
of glaciers, time-tides of ice, mastodons,
saber-toothed tigers, men with flint-tipped spears.
Then let the ice retreat, renew the rites
of spring, bring back thunder lizards and fronds
of towering ferns and cycads, fill clear,
warm inland seas with sharks and trilobites.

for Jason Mark

Reptiles

Evolve? We'll evolve when we want to. We're
reptiles—we decide. No mother love, no
promises—that's the deal. Don't get too near,
don't think too hard, don't ever think we owe
you anything, 'cause we don't. Where were you
when we hatched? You, who never saw our shells,
one perfect world piled on another—blue,
brown, green—it's true: we made our way. To hell
with your nipples, your kindergartens, your
wedding bells, golden rings—we'll show you rings.
We'll show you claws, too—remember? The more
you hurt, the more we—nothing. Go ahead, sing—
we don't do music, don't do memories—
why, when we'll outlast you? We don't do fair/
unfair. And we don't do thermostasis.
Go ahead, cry—we're reptiles, we don't care.

The Solitude of the Loris

Unseen in the unmoving trees, I smell
their fear, all those skittering little creatures
down there, darting hole to hole. I see
them press their luck, and lose. I hear them tell
the end of their stories in squeals and shrieks
and then they die. Meanwhile my goggle-eyed
attention is complete, serene — I hide
in stillness, glory in my slow, meticulous
unfolding. Why would you disturb
my unnerving silence? Why risk my bite —
so foul, so unforgettable? The night
is fatal to impatience. Unperturbed,
unhurried, I'm secure in the dark. Don't
vex yourself — why not just leave me alone?

The Audacity of the Jaguar

My world is not your world. Who was here first?
And who is the master? My amber eyes,
they're voiceless mirrors—imagine the worst
of me, call me coward, devil, beast. Why

should I burden myself with your fears? You
peer into these eyes and see nothing that
you know beyond your own reflection. Who
are you now? My wanderings are no matter

of yours—if you gaze into my coat
of a thousand eyes, I melt into smoke,
into spirit, into memory. Go
to bed now, lie beside your wife. That low

cough—just her soft snoring? Sleep. Dream your dreams
of all that you will do with fences, fire—
your farm, your *finca*—oh, how it all seems
to be yours. And when you awaken, I

recede and I wait and I watch until
you send your shadow man. And I'll remain
here, hidden, choosing what I want to kill.
Closer—I can bite you through to the brain.

for Alan Rabinowitz

IV

LEXICON

Words Fail

Metaphors miss it, the way spring comes on—
Vermont in April, after sugaring,
winter's wrack laid bare — the snows are gone

and then the mud gives way to the *more more*
more of May—life! — the return of the sun
and every shade of green, the quiet roar

of the forest. The insistence of spring
is not art, not a song or a poem or
a picture— it's not like anything.

Green

Spring in New England — a violence of green,
sudden, hysterical verdure, a paint
bomb blast leaving everything drenched in green
that burns, that renders absurd the last faint
faltering memory of winter, green
of every shade, depth, tint, mood, height, and hue,
the fresh, blinking-itself-to-life green
we call tender, velvet green that tells you
why they made the money green, urgent green
mad for the sun, for photosynthesis,
for the alchemies of summertime, green
to resurrect the dead, green to twist
your heart with envy that you are not green,
not anymore, not like this — not like this.

From Windmill Hill

Money done right— who can say no? I mean,
the view from here: first God made Monadnock,
faraway blue floating on evening green,

a sapphire set in jade, the big fat book
of beauty— but money made it a view,
money cut a thousand trees, said, *There, look,*

away beyond the Connecticut: Beauty.
Money well spent, says me. Money's just
a dream of what it would be like to do

something, make something, be something. The lust
for money is ugly, everyone knows
that— we know it in our bones, in the dust

of what didn't work, fell short, was supposed
to deliver and didn't— innocence betrayed
and costing far too much. These maples, though—

that mountain, those clouds— what if money made
God, and God made this solstice, set this scene
for us to be worthy of beauty, and we obeyed?

Cutting the Grass

I tell myself I'm farming—who's to say
I'm not? My crop is meditations: on
blood-borne memories of scything the hay
in County Cork . . . on wasted labor . . . on
the void, fruitless expenditure of time . . .
on summer's exuberant duties . . . on
the seventh-day semiotics of trim,
orderly boundaries, nature at bay . . . on
the ordeals of beauty, beer-tempered heat
and bugs and weeds and choices and the meaning
of the slow, soft encroachment of night.
But I'm no farmer—I'm a fireman, beating
my righteous blades against this quiet green
inferno that burns at the speed of light.

In the Woods

It can happen when you walk in the woods—
not always, sometimes, and once is enough:
you see the invisible forest, the stuff
between. Sometimes the trees are buried, shouldering
last night's snow, everywhere is silent,
still. Then a soft rumble as a pine
drops its burden all at once, and a fine
white cloud thumps heavily down, and meanwhile
nothing is perturbed, silence is restored.
Again, the stillness. Or in summer, when
the woods throb and the light of the sun drives
the season's teeming madness, and the more
you look, the more you see it, unspoken,
shimmering around everything alive.

Edges (October Twilight)

Let others bicker over who made what—
isn't everybody making? Aren't we
made for making—building, devising? But
more than that—looking for some kind of freedom
for later, some kind of heaven? I
look for it in this forest, at the edge
between summer and winter, day and night.
I look for it in tidepools, at the edge
between the sea and the land, between strange
and stranger. I look for it where the flats
meet the mountains. The edges are the welfare
of the world, the crucibles of change
and chance, the portals between this and that—
the pockets where the world creates itself.

Living with Cold

Winter begins in July, when the days
are long but getting shorter, when the green
world rushes toward fulfillment, when the haze
of a hot afternoon no longer means
that summer is forever. We've been told
before: there's an art to living with cold.

Winter is the soul of autumn, the ghost
in October's machine — no more pretending
there's nothing to prepare, not when most
of the leaves have turned. Everything depends
on what we do now — will the woodshed hold
enough? There's an art to living with cold.

Winter begins as absence, dwindling glow
of the sun, alarming onrush of night
and everything darkness means. When the snow
comes in the hush of December, the rites
of time are rattled in with beech leaves rolled
up tight. There's an art to living with cold.

Winter is old news by February,
but winter doesn't care about our comfort,
doesn't care about our bones, and we
do well to forget, let ourselves grow numb
to color, value silver over gold,
and master the art of living with cold.

Whiteout

In the blizzard we were zombies, the few
of us still moving, still stumbling toward
the places we belonged. I figured you

for dead at first, you with your hands so cold,
your eyes so blankly frozen. Was it true,
what you murmured into my ear? You told

me how you hated the wind, how the hard,
dark months forced their fingers into the old
hurts, old wounds, how healed doesn't mean unscarred.

Through the Soil

The problem is the prison of our words—
if we call it *talk*, that thing that trees do
through their roots, we render the thought absurd
and blind ourselves to a fresh kind of beauty.
So call it something else, then—this chemical
communication, this exchange
of intricate knowledge, many Decembers
and just as many Mays, all the strange
ways of soil and sunlight.
                              Words are the pins
that pierce the butterflies of what we mean,
displaying them as lifeless at the instant
that we speak. So how to say it—between
the fluttering and the net, or the truth
in the dirt, the message that must go through?

A Wider Lens

I guess I'm no photographer. I tried
to take a picture (a paltry ambition,
this desire to take, bag trophies, hide
behind the lens), but the thing that I wished
for wasn't a thing at all. I got beauty
as glimpsed through a porthole, but that's not
how it looked from the crow's nest, where the view
was limitless. If my camera caught
the glare of the sun, it was just by accident —
the light was alive and elusive.
Where was the oceanic swell, the gentle
rolling of the sea? I got the fact
but not the feel, and no hint of the dues
I'd paid to get there, or what it all meant.

The Music Inside

Most people go to their graves
with their music still in them.

—Benjamin Disraeli

No one wants to die with their music still
silent. No—I want my very last note
to ring like church bells on Easter, to fill
my heart with love and forgiveness, to float
in the air like smoke, weightless, final, true.
Imagine: you're on a bus, everyone
sits tuneless, pretending silence, but you
can hear their hearts, inner symphonies running
wild to the rhythm of the world, heedless
of their rough harmonies, overtones
of life. We're all on that bus, we're all pleading
our cases in a court made of bones
while our souls are singing, filling the air
with all we are, always and everywhere.

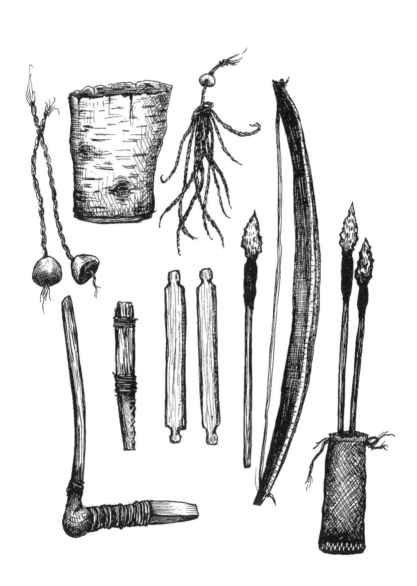

NOTES

"On the Bus" — Thanks to Jon Krakauer, author of *Into the Wild*, for telling us how Chris McCandless lived and died, and to Tom Wolfe, author of *The Electric Kool-Aid Acid Test*, for telling us how Ken Kesey and his Merry Pranksters boarded their psychedelic bus, Furthur, and set out on the long, strange trip that so many of us have been on ever since.

"Saint David's Head" — The relentless west wind that blows across the Irish Sea is the voice of the spectral wraiths of Irish lore, the banshees, not their Welsh counterparts, the cyhyraeths.

"Math Teacher" — In siSwati, *umlumbi* means "white person."

"Pedestal" — Don Sheehan was the longtime executive director and guiding light of The Frost Place Poetry Festival, held annually in Franconia, New Hampshire.

"Ötzi" — In 1991, Europe's oldest-known natural mummy, along with an array of Stone Age weapons and tools, was discovered in a melting glacier in the Ötzal Alps between Italy and Austria. He was dubbed "Ötzi the Iceman." Forensic investigators revealed that, about five thousand years ago, he died there of numerous wounds; an arrowhead was embedded in his shoulder.

"Rewilding the Golf Course" — Thanks to Jason Mark, author of *Satellites in the High Country: Searching for the Wild in the Age of Man.*

"The Audacity of the Jaguar" — Thanks to Alan Rabinowitz, author of *An Indomitable Beast: The Remarkable Journey of the Jaguar.*

"Through the Soil" — German forester Peter Wohlleben has described the way trees "talk" to each other in his book *The Hidden Life of Trees: What They Feel, How They Communicate.*

ACKNOWLEDGMENTS

Many thanks to those who have welcomed me into the world of living poetry, especially Tom Rea, Helen Barkan, Patti Blanco, Meg Kearney, Jett Whitehead, Peter Wood, David Keller, Don Sheehan, Wyn Cooper, Suzanne Kingsbury, Baron Wormser, and Vievee Francis, and to those who helped me with the manuscript— Chard deNiord, Frances Cannon, Neil Shepard, Rebecca Starks, and Diana Whitney. And special thanks to Frances Cannon, director of the Sundog Poetry Center, for her savvy, her enthusiasm, and her original artwork (as well as the cover photo), to Dede Cummings, founder of Green Writers Press, for the great book design, and to Elizabeth Ungerleider for braving a bitterly cold January morning to take the author photo.

I have had the great good fortune to be awarded fellowships from Ragdale Foundation, Virginia Center for the Creative Arts, Dorland Mountain Arts Colony, Ucross Foundation, and Vermont Studio Center.

Finally, I am grateful to the editors of the following publications, in which a number of these poems first appeared:

Atlanta Review: "Rewilding the Golf Course"

Crosswinds: "Vichy"

Helen: "Casino," "Play Me the Blues"

The Salon: "Math Teacher"

Sandcutters: "Dreaming of Socrates," "Hungry"

Sixfold: "The Audacity of the Jaguar," "Jubilee Blues," "On the Bus," "Reptiles," "Saint David's Head," "Waiting in Line at the Liquor Store"

Southword: "The Merry Dancers," "Perfect"

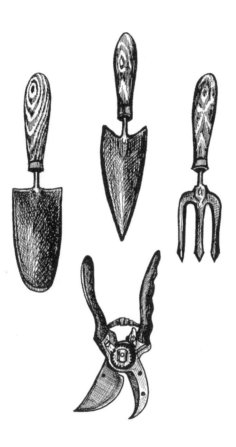

ABOUT THE AUTHOR

PHOTO BY ELIZABETH UNGERLEIDER

MICHAEL FLEMING was born in San Francisco, raised in Wyoming, and has lived and learned and worked all around the world, from Thailand, England, and Swaziland to Berkeley, New York City, and now Brattleboro, Vermont. He's been a teacher, a grad student, a carpenter, a musician, and always a writer; for the past twenty years he has edited books of every description.

CPSIA information can be obtained
at www.ICGtesting.com
Printed in the USA
JSHW021935150623
43315JS00002B/103

9 781950 584840